FLAMINGO KNEES

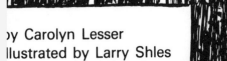

by Carolyn Lesser
Illustrated by Larry Shles

Oakwood Press
St. Louis

FLAMINGO KNEES

Flamingo knees,
    Flamingo toes,
        Flamingo beak,
            Flamingo woes.

MUFFIN

Lippety-lippety, wiggle and twitch,
Ears trailing over the ground,
Softly, silently, muffled in fluff,
The lops are coming to town.

Quietly, quietly, watching with hope,
My eyes loving each one I see,
Softly, silently, muffled in fluff,
The brown one hops over to me.

Cuddling, cuddling, nestle and snooze,
He snuggles with me night and day.
Softly, silently, muffled in fluff,
That lop stole my heart away.

GREAT CRYSTAL BEAR

Snow-cold bear,
Alone
Padding across ice floes,
Where is your bed?

Is it a drift of silver snow
In the starry night?
Are the light-curtains waving
In the midnight sky your blankets?
Who tucks you in polar bear?

Snow-cold bear,
Alone
On the ice,
Where are your friends?

Are they chilly little fishes
In the icy sea,
Leaping just out of reach
Playing tag,
As your mighty webbed paws
Swim you from lunch to dinner?
Who listens to your dream-wishes?

Oh great and wise-eyed
Crystal bear,
I would like to know your secrets
For cold
And
Alone.

MY WISH

If I were as powerful
As an Eastern sage,
I would rob the world
Of hate and rage.

Then no one big
Could hurt anyone
Small.
We'd hug and love,
And laugh,
That's all.

SHY

The big soft panda was plopped on a hill,
A mound of shy gentleness sitting still.
I hope when he peeked through that
Stand of bamboo,
He saw I was shy and gentle too.

If I were bold,
I would snuggle and giggle,
Might kiss his nose,
Tweek his ears 'til they wiggle.

But since we're both quiet
And frightfully shy,
We'll wave and smile
Then say
Good-bye.

LIFE IN A POCKET

Life in a pocket
Is a life that I love.
I fit in mom's pocket
Like a hand in a glove.
I don't need to hop,
I don't need to run.
I bounce with my mom
Having in-pocket fun.

But pocket-life is
A life made for two.
Two have to do
What just one wants to do.
I want to check out
That creek sparkling blue.
But now mom wants lunch,
So it's kangaroo stew.

Just for this moment,
While I am still small,
Mom's toasty warm pocket
Feels best of all.
So, I'll wait and I'll hope
That when I am free,
That sparkling blue creek
Has waited for me.

TWIRLING PEARL

There was a flamingo named Pearl,
Who dreamed she could dance
With a twirl.
But try as she might,
Her moves just weren't right
For her knees bent the wrong way,
Poor girl.

WHY NOT KNOT?

When she heard the music she couldn't resist.
Rockin' and rollin' Pearl did the twist.
Heart beatin' fast, filled with delight,
She swiveled and swirled into the night.

When morning dawned she went to school,
Still twistin' and twirlin', feelin' cool.
"Your neck's in a knot!" laughed all her friends.
"So what!" said Pearl. "I love my bends!"

SOARING TO SASKATOON

Seven bats upside-down
Hanging high and brave.
Tiny toes tug at rocks
In the coal-black cave.

Seven bats wake and shake
Stretching claws and wings
Swoosh into the starlight
Squeeking...ping! ting! zing!

Seven bats in a line
Dance around the moon,
Float and flip, dive and dip,
Then soar to Saskatoon!

TUESDAY NIGHT

The lights went out, the moon shone bright,
That fateful, frightful Tuesday night.
They saw her there, in her bed,
Body skiny, hair bright red,
Mary Margaret saying prayers.

They slipped in hushed over the sill,
Stood in a line, watching her.......still.
Sparkling eyes gazed big and bright
At Mary Margaret in silver light.
Then one sneezed!

The sneeze and the sparkle from their eyes
Startled her, caught her by surprise.
Mary Margaret sat up, heart beating fast,
Clutched her bear, stared and gasped.
Monsters! Thought Mary Margaret.
There are Monsters in my room!

A Monster! whispered the whole line of them, terrified.
There is a gigantic Monster in this weird place!

In that single moment of blackest night
Fear filled the room, packed it tight.
Terror stalked, taking the air,
While no one...nothing...moved.

Then Mary Margaret shivered a bit,
Blinked and gluped the air.
She winked at them, smiled and whispered
"You're cute! You're everywhere!"

Little did she know her winks and blinks
Were their signs of friendship and meeting.
For suddenly the whole line of them
Did a wonderful dance of greeting.
Over and under, around the bed
They swirled and twirled over her head.
Then Mary Margaret asked, "May I dance too?"

In the moonlight all of them played and laughed
'Til Mary Margaret heard feet on the stair.
"Hide!" she hissed, jumping in bed.
Her mom said, "Mary Margaret, who's there?"
Mary Margaret was taught never to lie
So she told the truth without fear.
"A line of monsters invaded my room!"
Said her mom, "What an imagination, my dear!"

But Mary Margaret saw lights in her dollhouse
Sparkling from their bright, twinkly eyes.
She beamed and blinked, whispered and winked,
"Thanks for the wonderfully frightful,
Simply delightful,
Great Tuesday night surprise!"

LOW SPOTS, HIGH SPOTS

Spots in the jungle hide in a tree,
Slink through vines, silently.
Spots enclose a smile that scares,
Eyes that frighten with chilling stares.

Spots leave footprints huge, behind,
From paws that fight, paws unkind.
Spots surrounding slitty eyes
Belong to silent, lurking spies!
Jaguars!

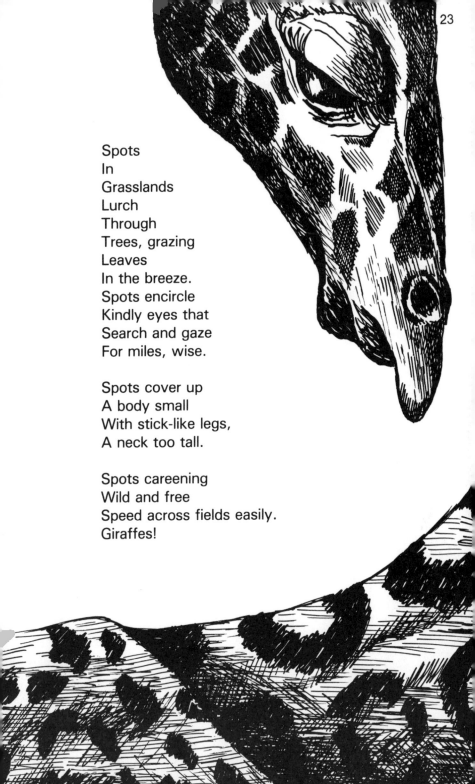

Spots
In
Grasslands
Lurch
Through
Trees, grazing
Leaves
In the breeze.
Spots encircle
Kindly eyes that
Search and gaze
For miles, wise.

Spots cover up
A body small
With stick-like legs,
A neck too tall.

Spots careening
Wild and free
Speed across fields easily.
Giraffes!

FOLLOW ME

Attention! Attention! Get in line!
Class will start at half-past nine.
You'll learn to slide and dive, watch me.
You'll love the ice, the sparkling sea.

Annie, Zack, Jennifer, Kate,
Stacy, Beth, Timothy, Nate,
Exercises first, raise flippers, hup!
For heaven's sake, DeWayne, stand up.

Right and left, then one, two, three.
Look over here! Follow me!
You'll never swim or strut or bow
If you don't watch. You won't know how.

My teaching is a flop today.
Perhaps it's time for me to play.
I'm diving in, this swim feels fine!
Wow! Here they come! My penguin line!

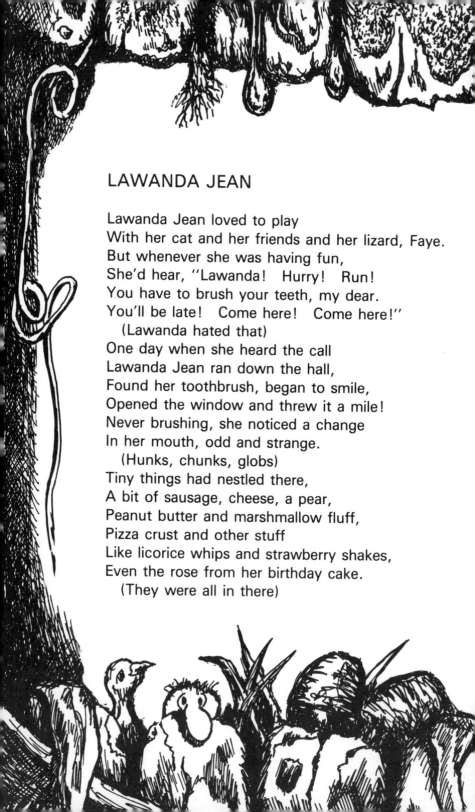

LAWANDA JEAN

Lawanda Jean loved to play
With her cat and her friends and her lizard, Faye.
But whenever she was having fun,
She'd hear, "Lawanda! Hurry! Run!
You have to brush your teeth, my dear.
You'll be late! Come here! Come here!"
  (Lawanda hated that)
One day when she heard the call
Lawanda Jean ran down the hall,
Found her toothbrush, began to smile,
Opened the window and threw it a mile!
Never brushing, she noticed a change
In her mouth, odd and strange.
  (Hunks, chunks, globs)
Tiny things had nestled there,
A bit of sausage, cheese, a pear,
Peanut butter and marshmallow fluff,
Pizza crust and other stuff
Like licorice whips and strawberry shakes,
Even the rose from her birthday cake.
  (They were all in there)

Her cave-dark mouth became a spot
Where teeny things began to rot.
First a paste, then a goo
Began to ooze, greenish-blue.
It crept all through her mouth one night,
By morning it was a ghastly sight!
   (Her teeth were slimy)
Lawanda Jean grew very mean
When people shrieked, "Your teeth!   They're green!"
She wanted to kick, she wanted to bite,
To hit and scratch, to fight and fight!
Friends wouldn't play, the cat wouldn't purr.
It was no secret, her teeth were fur.
   (She was lonely)
Then on a blue-sky, sunny day
Lawanda breathed, "Good morning, Faye!"
The lizard looked up, then reeled and fell
Flat on her face in the revolting smell.
Lawanda stared, then began to cry,
"My very last friend is about to die!"
   (It's all my fault!)
Rushing away, she ran to the sink,
Brushed the sludge away in a wink.
Breathing mint in and out,
She revived dear Faye, danced her about,
Called her friends, tickled her cat,
Smiled at her parents,
And that was that!

MAXIM'S BEAT

Let's hear it for tap shoes!
Those chit-chatting slippers,
The click-clacks, the spin-slaps,
Like fin-whacks of kippers.

That cha-cha-thwack-splat-tic-
Flap-cha-cha-tic-tapping,
Clap-cha-cha-thwack-splat-tic-
Flap-cha-cha-tic-tapping!

Bravissimo, tap shoes!
With glitzy spark-spangles,
With fluffed bows all sequins,
With shiny clack-jangles.

Wild cheers for the tap shoes!
Crowding click-snaps in rooms,
But they're best on kids' feet
Making magic!
VA-VOOM!

A RAINBOW NAMED IGOR

Hi, Mom! I'm calling from
The pet shop.
Mom.... how would you like
To live with a
Rainbow?
This guy came to school today.
He brought an iguana.
Beautiful colors!
Blue-green changing to
Lime... all iridescent.
Mom...they have iguanas
For sale here.
Can I get one?

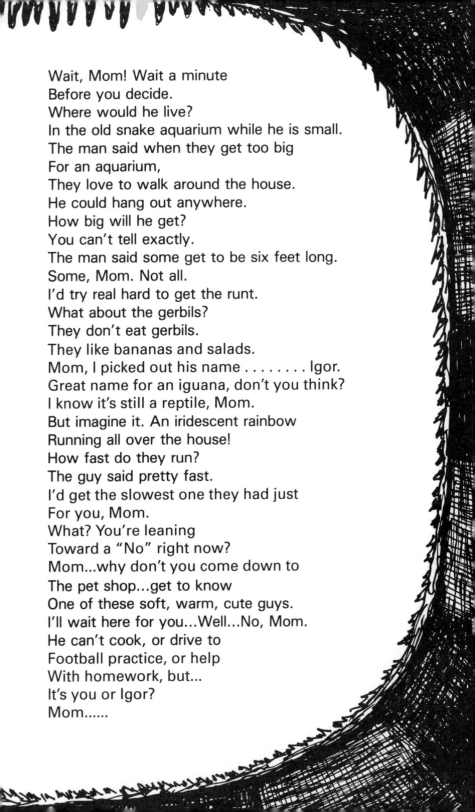

Wait, Mom! Wait a minute
Before you decide.
Where would he live?
In the old snake aquarium while he is small.
The man said when they get too big
For an aquarium,
They love to walk around the house.
He could hang out anywhere.
How big will he get?
You can't tell exactly.
The man said some get to be six feet long.
Some, Mom. Not all.
I'd try real hard to get the runt.
What about the gerbils?
They don't eat gerbils.
They like bananas and salads.
Mom, I picked out his name . . . . Igor.
Great name for an iguana, don't you think?
I know it's still a reptile, Mom.
But imagine it. An iridescent rainbow
Running all over the house!
How fast do they run?
The guy said pretty fast.
I'd get the slowest one they had just
For you, Mom.
What? You're leaning
Toward a "No" right now?
Mom...why don't you come down to
The pet shop...get to know
One of these soft, warm, cute guys.
I'll wait here for you...Well...No, Mom.
He can't cook, or drive to
Football practice, or help
With homework, but...
It's you or Igor?
Mom......

UPS AND DOWNS

I bought the yo-yo
'Cause the guy in the store
Said, "Be the Champ!"
"Be the King of your street!"

So I bought it and spun it,
And flipped it and flung it,
But, should "Champ" have it
Wrapped 'round his feet?

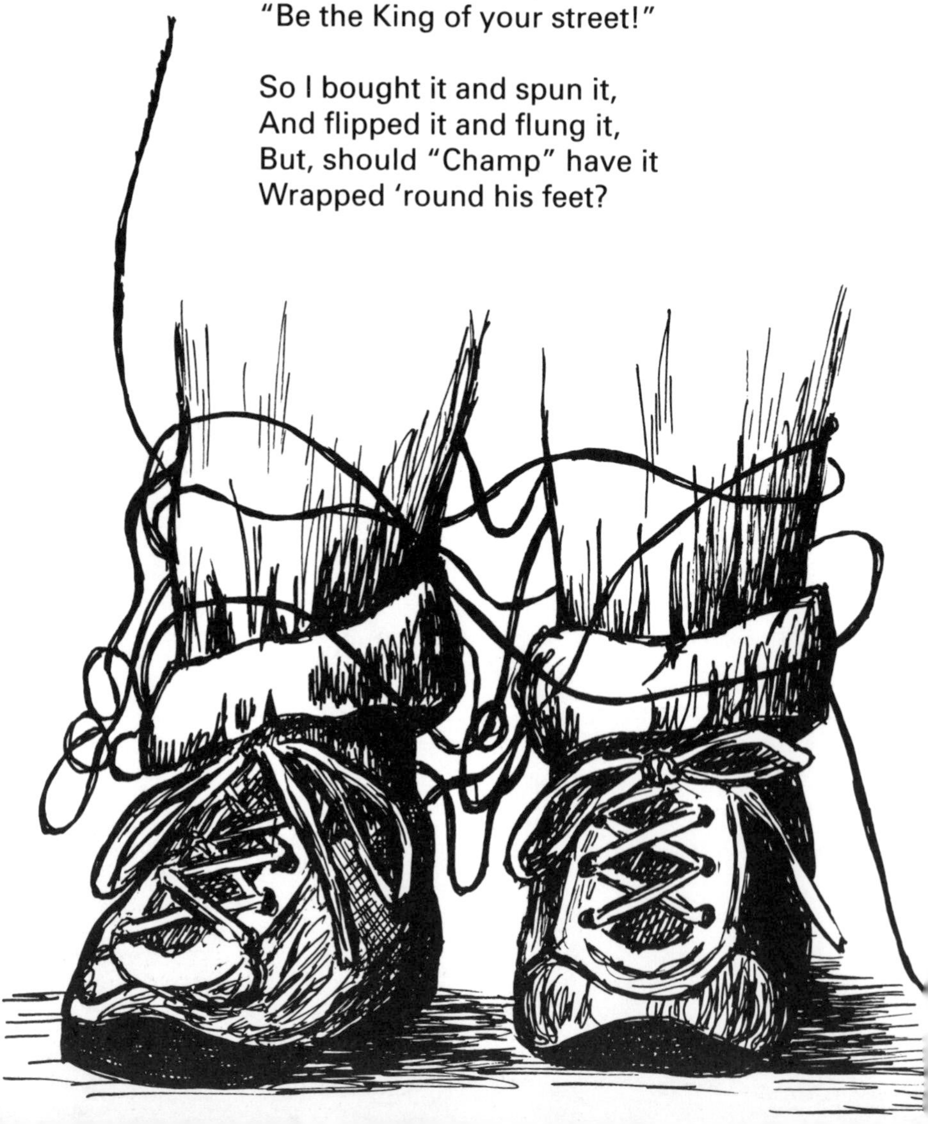

ALL MINE

"This kitten's all mine,"
I said to my brother, my father,
My sister, my friend, and my mother.

"The litterbox needs cleaning!"
Mom said, "Now, let's see...
Who owns that new kitten?"

"Anyone," I shouted,
"But me!"

SCHOOL LUNCH

At lunch Jason put the whole orange in his mouth,
While Pete made his tongue touch his nose.
Then Matt dumped his fries on his pizza real quick
And topped it with jello and rolls.
He gobbled great globs as Dale began burping
The tune to some top-twenty song.
Charlene strutted in with folded-back lids.
Her lashes were suddenly gone!

When Mike swaggered in, turned back his lips,
Making "war-noise" like dive-bombing planes.
Big Benjy strolled through with his "pit viper" look,
His tongue in a point, showing veins.
Then Joe stuffed the twenty saltines in his mouth,
Chris tried with twenty-one grapes.
Old Kevin blew up a balloon with his nose,
Making gross and incredible shapes!

Russell started rolling his eyeballs around
Until all you could see was white.
Antonio did his superb cross-eyed stare,
Lips stretched in a great vampire bite.
With straws in his nose, his mouth and his ears,
Jeffrey stood up looking "cool".
As Earl began his staccato-like chatter,
Firing bread crumbs, noodles and drool.

Jim ended the show by flaring his nostrils
At ninety-nine times in a minute.
And me, sitting here, what's my claim to fame?
Lunch starts, I say, "SHOWTIME! Begin it!!"

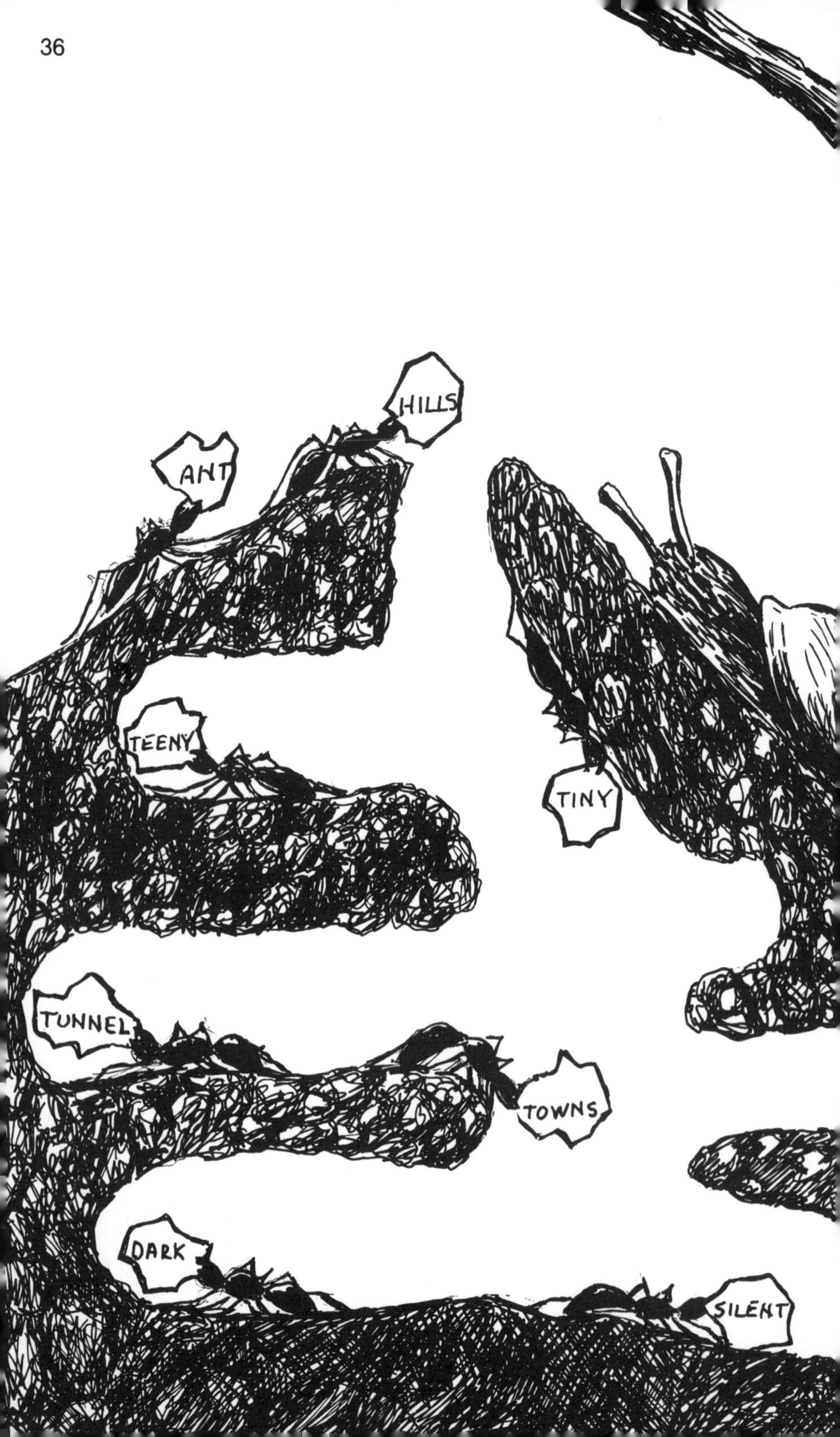

ANT

HILLS

TEENY

TINY

TUNNEL

TOWNS

DARK

SILENT

INCH BY INCH BY INCH BY INCH BY INCH BY INCH BY INCH BY INCH.

SLOWLY DAWDLING, IDLY CRAWLING, UNDER EASY SAIL, A SNAIL!

LIVES.

PERILOUS PEARL

BEWARE! ATTACK FLAMINGO!
Said the sign on the fence near the gate.
Mind racing, I stood there wondering,
Could an "attack flamingo" be great?

Could she turn you to stone with a piercing stare,
Her gaze sending shivers of fright,
Or strangle in stealth with that long, skinny neck,
Holding her victim too tight?

Maybe she'd kick with her tall, spindly legs
That bend backwards and form angles strange. Perhaps
She would slash with that weird, hook-like beak.
If she did, I'd jump out of her range.

While I stood there reading "ATTACK FLAMINGO",
I spotted the hole in the fence.
I ran to the slats, looked through amazed!
Attack flamingo? It just made no sense,

She was balancing calmly on one thread-thin leg,
Her head tucked under her wing.
With that neck like a hose and body of feathers,
Clearly she wouldn't hurt a thing!

But the sight of her there was so bizarre,
It made me chuckle and gasp.
The more I looked, the more I giggled,
Until I actually laughed!

Sticks and pink fluff? Pink fluff and sticks?
A danger to our town?
I couldn't stop. I laughed and laughed
And laughed 'til I fell down!

But as I hit the cold, hard ground,
I soon came to my senses
As I realized that none of us have
Strong enough defenses.
For silently, without a move, truly sound asleep,
That silly sight of sticks and fluff
Had knocked me off my feet.

So if you go out walking all around our town,
BEWARE! ATTACK FLAMINGO!
She'll laugh you to the ground!

Tulips touch tulips
In blue sky-shine, green Springtime
How lovely love is.

Brown toad under leaves
Can you hide from spying eyes?
Not from mine, you can't!

Chickadee clinging
to a breeze-blown sunflower bright.
Your carnival ride?

FOREST NIGHT

An eerie cry shrieks
Over the snow.
The sound
Hangs
In the crisp air
Like an icicle
On the edge of a branch.

In the black night
Silence drapes heavily
Over frosty trees
And frozen earth.
Slashing through the birches
And pines
Until another howl pierces
The night shadows.

Prowling on silent paws,
The wolves gather.

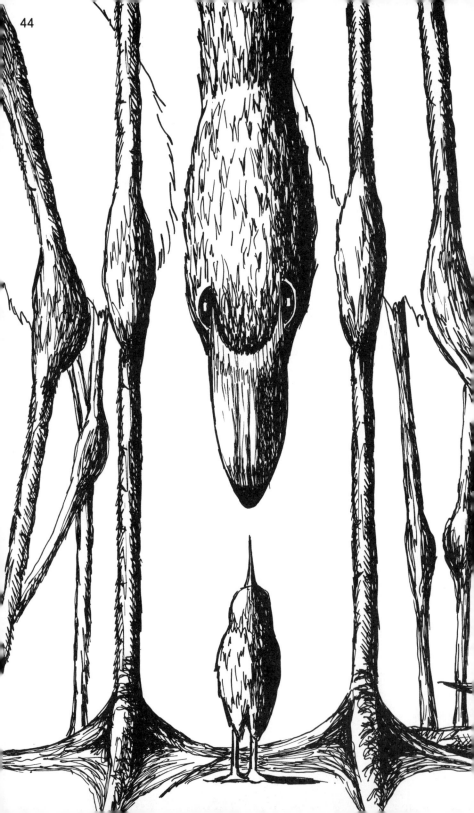

LOST

I'm a sandpiper
Lost in this forest.
Lost
In millions and zillions
Of trees.

What?
This isn't a forest?
You're flamingos?
These are your knees?

Here I stand
In knees and feet,
My heart set on learning
To fly,
To soar over waves
Riding the wind.

Will you help me
Find the sky?

STUCK

My friend and me, my friend and me,
We are stuck like glue, you see.
No matter what, no matter when,
He sticks to me, I stick to him.

If I am red and in a rage,
If he is blue with sad,
We stick and purple happens,
Changing mad and sad to glad.

We stumble in the shadows,
We dance in sunlight new,
My friend and me,
My friend and me are lucky.
We got glue!

ARTISTS' EYES

Artists' eyes feel the shape of things,
Tracing the edges and shadows and curves.
The remembering eyes store away
Light on the snow,
The curve of a cheek,
The shape and color of
Summer.

Artists' hearts so quickly grasp
The feeling of things seen,
They rush at paper or paint,
Clay or cloth,
Their hearts inspired
To show miracles of leaves,
The terror of wolves,
The power and grace of a storm.

Then eyes that feel and hearts inspired
Move hands.
Artists' hands see, as artists' hands dance,
Looping and swaying, drawing and sculpting,
Shapes following the path
Of their hands.
Artists conduct beauty from dreaming to waking.

Artists' eyes and hearts and hands
Give us ourselves new again,
Give us our world new again.
Artists remind us that beauty is here,
Now.

Gray-bleak February day.
  Geese flying North!
    In the sky..
  a thread of hope.

Red-orange ladybug
asleep on the gray gull's feather,
are your dreams of wings?

MOON DREAMS

When the moon came up and the lights got low,
Up to my room is where I'd go.
I pulled the covers over my head,
Grabbed book and flashlight and snuggled in bed.

Then mom would call, "Turn out your light!"
"Sure thing!" I answered, then grinned with delight
As my hand slipped under the pillow and then...
Click! Flashlight on, I'd be reading again.

My books were like carpets, flying free.
When I hopped aboard they carried me
To spooky castles and wild, distant shores.
I traveled through time, books opened the door.

But who were these "Gods" writing the books?
Writing the words that caused me to look,
That caused me to feel and made me see,
I could write too! There were stories in me!

Perhaps one day I could actually be
Writing books for children like you, like me.
Books read in bed, in the dark, by flashlight.
My dream came true. So can yours.
Goodnight!

52

INDEX